TRUMPET *signature licks*®

DIZZY GILLESPIE

by Artemis Music Ltd.

Cover photo provided by the Frank Driggs Collection

ISBN-13: 978-0-634-08216-0
ISBN-10: 0-634-08216-7

HAL•LEONARD® CORPORATION

7777 W. BLUEMOUND RD. P.O. BOX 13819 MILWAUKEE, WI 53213

Visit Hal Leonard Online at
www.halleonard.com

CONTENTS

INTRODUCTION

Dizzy Gillespie

(1917–1993)

Life and Recordings

John Birks Gillespie was born in Cheraw, South Carolina on October 21, 1917. His father was an amateur bandleader who tutored his son on several instruments, giving the young Dizzy a grounding in music. He died when Dizzy was just ten, but his son went on to pick up the trombone at the age of 12, moving on to the trumpet a couple of years later. Dizzy was largely self-taught, and although he studied harmony and theory at the Laurinburg Institute in North Carolina from 1932–35, he always preferred playing music to formal study.

He moved to Philadelphia in 1935 and began gigging with local bands. It was during this period that he earned the epithet "Dizzy" due to his zany onstage behavior with the Frankie Fairfax band. Dizzy's astonishing technique was already attracting a lot of attention, and in 1937, he travelled to New York where he got a job touring Europe with Teddy Hill, replacing his hero Roy Eldridge in the band.

When Teddy Hill disbanded his group, Gillespie joined the Cab Calloway band, where he first met the Cuban trumpeter Mario Bauza. This friendship was to inspire a life-long interest in Afro-Cuban rhythms. Also at this time, Dizzy recorded a solo on a Lionel Hampton tune called "Hot Mallets" which has been described as the first recorded example of bebop.

In 1940, Gillespie met Charlie Parker while on tour in Kansas City, and from 1941, he began attending late-night jam sessions at Minton's Playhouse and Clark Monroe's Uptown House with Parker, Kenny Clarke, Thelonious Monk, and others. Later that year, Dizzy was fired from the Calloway band following an on-stage fracas and subsequently went freelance, working with artists including Coleman Hawkins, Duke Ellington, Ella Fitzgerald, and Earl "Fatha" Hines. Important recordings from this period include his solo on Les Hite's "Jersey Bounce."

In early 1944, Gillespie recorded his original composition "Woodyn' You," which is another candidate for the first recorded example of bebop. Shortly afterwards he joined Billy Eckstine's new band as trumpeter and musical director. Designed as a backing group for Eckstine's new career as a singer, the group became more interested in developing bebop, and featured sidemen including Gene Ammons, Wardell Gray, Fats Navarro, and Miles Davis.

In 1945, Dizzy formed a quintet with Charlie Parker at the Three Deuces on 52nd Street which resulted in the seminal recordings "Hot House," "Shawnuff," and "Salt Peanuts." The other members of the quintet varied, but included Al Haig, Curley Russell, Sid Catlett, Milt Jackson, Ray Brown, and Stan Levey. After a brief stint in Hollywood, Gillespie returned to New York in 1946 to form his own bebop big band, which stayed together on and off for the next four years. Following a recommendation from his friend Mario Bauza, Gillespie employed the Cuban percussionist Chano Pozo, whose influence can be heard on the recording of their co-written original "Manteca." A 1947 recording contract with RCA ensured a steady income and enabled the group to stay together until 1950, after which time the rhythm section of John Lewis, Milt Jackson, Kenny Clarke, and Ray Brown went on to become the first incarnation of the Modern Jazz Quartet.

In the early fifties Dizzy toured briefly with Stan Kenton and formed his own record label (Dee Gee Records), which despite a hit ("Ooh-Shoo-Be-Doo-Bee"), was in financial problems by 1952. In 1953, an accident at a party for Dizzy's wife resulted in the bell of his trumpet being bent upwards. Dizzy tried playing the instrument, and paradoxically, found that he preferred the sound of the upswept bell and it soon became his trademark.

Throughout the fifties Dizzy toured with Jazz at the Philharmonic and recorded a succession of albums for Granz with a variety of different line-ups. In 1956 he took part in a U.S. State Department-sponsored tour of the Middle East and Africa which was successful enough to merit a follow-up tour later the same year to South America.

Dizzy continued to tour and record for the next three decades, with highlights including being placed on the ballot for President at the 1962 California Primary, a reunion tour with the big band in 1968, a world tour with the Giants of Jazz (1971–72), the "Tribute to Dizzy Gillespie" concert at Avery Fisher Hall (1975), and an appearance with his protégé Jon Faddis at the Montreux Jazz Festival (1977). In 1988, he formed the United Nations Orchestra, which toured Africa, Canada, and South America over the next three years.

Dizzy was involved in active music-making right up until his death in 1993, including a two-month residency at the Blue Note club in New York in 1992 with a series of all-star line-ups.

Style and Influence

Dizzy Gillespie was the first bebop trumpeter and has had wide-ranging influence on many instrumentalists, not just trumpet players. Gillespie was a virtuosic trumpeter in the same way as Louis Armstrong and Roy Eldridge, who were the main sources for his inspiration as a young player. Dizzy was affected most directly by Roy Eldridge, who was in turn strongly influenced by the playing of Louis Armstrong.

Roy Eldridge developed swing trumpet playing by emulating the long melodic lines and chord-based style of swing saxophonists such as Coleman Hawkins. Gillespie adopted many features of Eldridge's improvising style and applied them to the daring new harmonic ideas that he had developed with alto saxophonist Charlie Parker. Early in his career Gillespie often played with a cup mute, as did Eldridge, and would play spectacular high-note endings to some songs (such as "Groovin' High"). This was something that both Eldridge and Armstrong had employed.

Gillespie was very comfortable playing in the extreme upper register and would often unexpectedly leap up an octave in the middle of a phrase. This aspect, combined with his advanced rhythmic concepts, made his playing wild and unpredictable. He liked to play heavily-syncopated phrases, contrasted by fast flurries of notes that were often unrelated to the tempo, and liked to use intricate cross-rhythms. This interest in rhythm was also reflected in his involvement in Afro-Cuban music. Gillespie was very impressed by the playing and writing of Cuban trumpet player and arranger Mario Bauza, with whom he played in the Cab Calloway band when Dizzy was starting out as a professional musician. As a result, he began experimenting with the fusion of jazz and Cuban music in the mid-1940s with percussionist Chano Pozo, and wrote pieces such as "Manteca" for his Cuban-inspired big band.

Dizzy was an accomplished pianist (he actually plays piano on some Charlie Parker recordings) and developed a sophisticated approach to jazz harmony which employed much use of chord substitutions and extensions. This is reflected in the subtle chord sequences to his composition "Con Alma," as well as in his improvising. He would often end phrases on unexpected intervals or with notes that were very dissonant to the underlying harmony. Gillespie also created tension in his solos by holding long notes which were extremely dissonant to the chord but became consonant when the rhythm section harmony changed. The angular and wide intervals in his lines could be seen to be derived from piano voicings rather than the more scalar playing that was common with swing trumpeters. When Gillespie did use scales, he often employed unusual scales such as the diminished or whole tone.

Humor also played a big part in his music, and his playful quoting of all sorts of tunes was common (such as his use of a theme from Bizet's "Carmen" on "Hot House") as well as his singing on tunes such as "Salt Peanuts." Dizzy looked very striking when playing, partly because of the unusual upturned bell of his trumpet, but also because of the way that his cheeks would expand enormously when he played. However, in his later years this had a negative effect on his trumpet sound and flexibility because of the strain it put on his embouchure.

Gillespie had a strong influence on a younger generation of trumpet players, particularly Jon Faddis and Arturo Sandoval—whom he nurtured and encouraged—but above all, he changed the course of modern jazz for all instrumentalists through his advanced rhythmic and harmonic concepts, his championing of Cuban music, and his famous compositions such as "Night in Tunisia," "Con Alma," and "Manteca."

THE RECORDING

Mark White: trumpet
Tom Cawley: piano
Mark Hodgson: bass
Tom Gordon: drums

Note: All analyses refer to printed music for B♭ trumpet—not concert pitch—unless mentioned otherwise. In the event that any bass, piano, or guitar parts are written out, these will be written at sounding pitch (not transposed for trumpet).

ANTHROPOLOGY
(*The Complete RCA Victor Recordings 1937–1949, 1946*)

By Charlie Parker and Dizzy Gillespie

"Anthropology," composed by Dizzy with Charlie Parker, is one of numerous bebop tunes based on the chord progression from George Gershwin's "I Got Rhythm" (the so-called "rhythm changes"). The bridge had a different melody in an earlier incarnation of "Anthropology" entitled "Thriving on a Riff."

Dizzy plays the melody with cup mute (coupled with vibraphone), but blows open for his solo, which begins with a quote from "We're in the Money" (measures 33–36). The first eight measures draw from the C major scale, except the chromatic lower neighbor (D♯) in measure 39. Dizzy uses a Lydian (raised) 4th in measure 41 for C7 (see the F♯ on beat 3) and continues with C Lydian ♭7 (plus a D♭ chromatic passing tone) in the next measure. He shifts to C major with the B♮ on the downbeat of measure 43 going to an anticipation of D minor in the latter half of that measure with the presence of the F approached chromatically from G♭. In the second half of measure 44, the B♭ functions as the ♯9 of G7, although the entire measure could be analyzed as C Mixolydian. The F7 chord's E♭ arrives in the second half of measure 46, followed by a B♮ (written C♭), which implies the tritone substitute B major.

Measures 47–48 return to C Lydian ♭7 with the half-note F♯ (♯4) tying over to the bridge to become the 9th of E7 (measure 49). The 13th (C♯) shifts to ♭13th (C♮) on the way down the essentially E Mixolydian scale treatment of measure 49, followed by a G♯°7 outline in measure 50 (yielding the ♭9th). A7 is anticipated at the end of measure 50, and the ♯4 (D♯) is again featured in measure 51. The ♭7th (C) shifts to the major 7th (the leading tone C♯) in measure 53 for D7, and the C♯ is targeted again in measure 55. A blistering chromatic riff flutters between the 3rd (E) and 5th (G) of C7 throughout measures 57–59. That leads to a falling B♭ major scale for D7 and G7 in measure 60, but once again C7 (C Mixolydian) governs throughout a long phrase and series of changes (measures 61–62). The final two measures of the solo feature C Mixolydian decorated by chromatic neighbor tones.

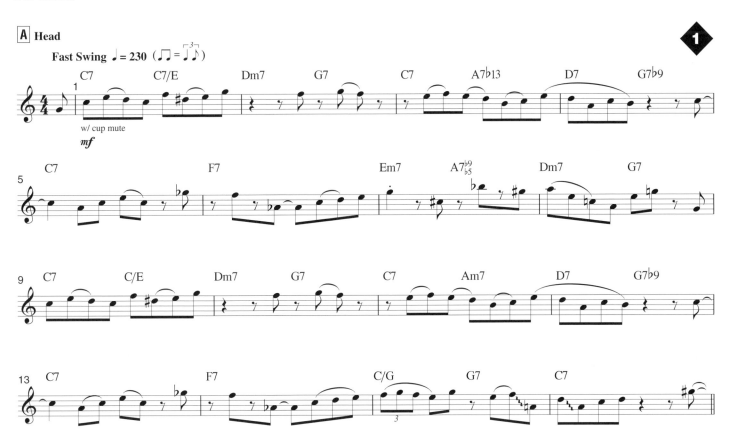

CON ALMA
(*Afro*, 1954)

By John "Dizzy" Gillespie

"Con Alma" is perhaps the most expressive and harmonically sophisticated of Dizzy's well-known compositions. After a four-bar intro consisting of alternating E♭9 and D9 chords, the tonality is established in G♭ major with a series of chords and inversions that create a descending bass line: G♭–B♭7/F–E♭m–E♭m7/D♭. Measure 7 marks the first departure from the diatonic bass line with C7, which is temporarily resolved to F in measure 8. By way of a chromatic passing E7 chord, the entire sequence starts over a minor 3rd lower with E♭ in measure 9.

Dizzy goes double time (syncopated sixteenths) for the first eight measures of the solo. There is an anticipation of C7 on beat 4 of measure 24 and an anticipation of F on beat 4 of measure 25. A bluesy ♭5 is featured in measure 28 for Cm followed by descending chromaticism into a little C Dorian melodic turn to get to the downbeat of A7 in measure 29. Notice the C♯°7 bop riff starting on the "and" of beat 2 that yields the ♭9 (B♭). The next eight measures are single time feel and include an implied G7♭9 (V of C7) in the second half of measure 32. There is good use of the ♯5th, ♭9th, and ♯9th over A7 in measure 37 via an F major scale fragment (built on the ♯5 of A).

In the bridge, a double-time D Locrian is used through most of the Dm7♭5–G7 (measures 39–40). Dizzy broadens the feel with quarter-note triplets in measures 43–44. In the last eight measures, the diminished 7th bebop riff returns (E° outlined in measure 49), followed by another F major anticipation (beat 4 of measure 49). Eighth- and quarter-note triplets wind down the close of the chorus, which ends with an A7♭9 extension on beat 1 of the final D major measure (54).

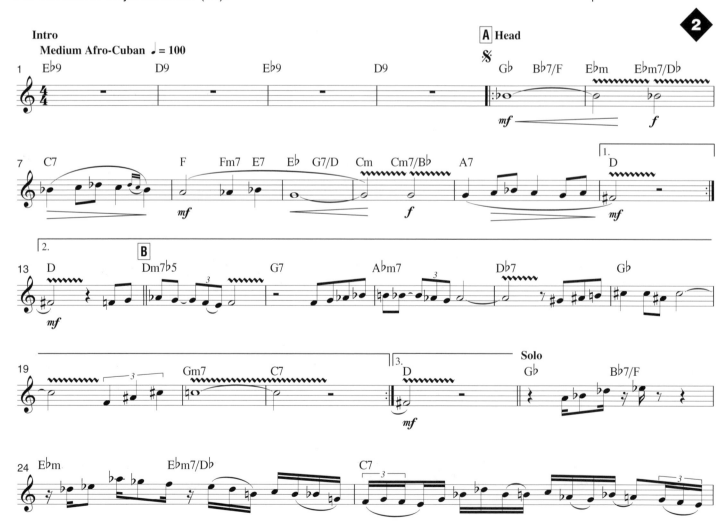

DIZZY ATMOSPHERE
(*Shawnuff*, 1945)

By John "Dizzy" Gillespie

The eponymous "Dizzy Atmosphere" (from the 1945 LP *Shawnuff* with Charlie Parker) is another well-known jazz standard composed by John "Dizzy" Gillespie. A thirty-two-measure AABA construction in B♭, it contains a descending chromatic bridge progression that bears a kinship with the work of fellow bebop composer Thelonious Monk (i.e., the bridge of "Well You Needn't").

Dizzy's cup-muted solo starts high, with the use of descending chromaticism (measure 37) and diatonic scales (measures 38 and 39) as well as chord outlines (40), altered tones (♭9, the A♭, for G7 in measure 39), suspensions (A♭ to G via the lower chromatic neighbor F♯ in measure 42), and encircling chromatic neighbors (F♯ and E into F at the downbeat of measure 43, and E♭–C♯–D later in that measure). He nails a double high B♭ (the tonic) in measure 46 and uses G, G♭, and E again in the second half of measure 50, suggesting an E° substitution. Notice the E sustaining over into measure 51, where it becomes the ♭5 (♯11) of B♭ major.

In the bridge, Dizzy uses a very high ♭9–root move over E7 in measure 54, and then echoes the two-note motif in the next measure. Double (two sets of) encircling chromatic neighbors (ECNs) appear in the second half of measure 56, and D♭7 and C7 each get one set of ECNs (G♭–E–F and F–E♭–E, respectively, in measures 58 and 59). In the first half of the final eight-measure section, a brilliant chromatic triplet passage emphasizes the different contexts of the notes G and F (and later E♭ and D) taken through a series of chord changes. G functions as the 13th for B♭ major, the root for G7, and the 5th for Cm7 in measures 61 and 62.

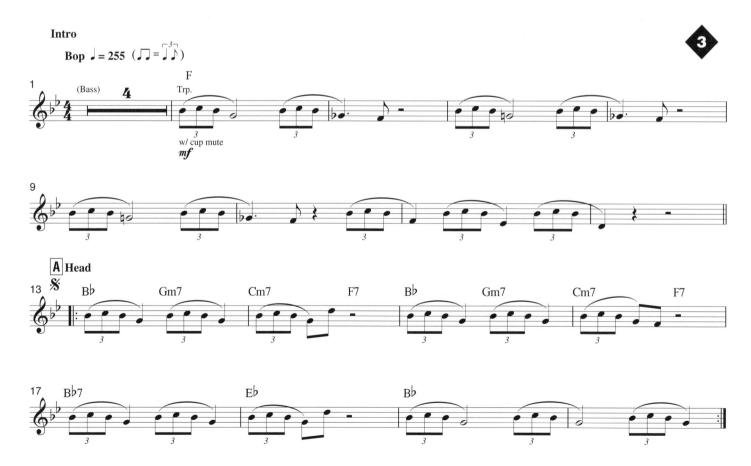

GROOVIN' HIGH
(*Shawnuff*, 1945)

By John "Dizzy" Gillespie

"Groovin' High" was penned by Dizzy and recorded in 1945 when he co-led a group with Charlie Parker. It is one of the classic tunes that first established Dizzy as a significant composer in the new bebop style.

In measure 24 (solo break), Dizzy uses the ♭7 immediately following the band's F6/9 downbeat. Towards the end of the break (from the "and" of beat 2, measure 26), he plays an F♯7 substitution (a half step above the chord change), and in measure 27 on beat 3, he outlines a V7 (C7♯11) to set up the return to F. In measure 30 he employs the ♭9 with the G♯°7 arpeggio; measure 34 features a similar treatment with A°7. In measure 35, the F on beat 4 is an anticipation of the G7 chord of the next measure. In that measure (36), the ♯11 is obtained via a Dm9 (maj7) arpeggio, with a nice syncopation on the "and" of beat 2 (third triplet note). The first three notes of measure 39 are upper and lower chromatic neighbors into the 3rd of C7. A leading tone precedes an Fmaj9 arpeggio in measure 40, which extends into measure 41 (first two notes), arriving at the ♭9 (E♭) of a D7 substitution.

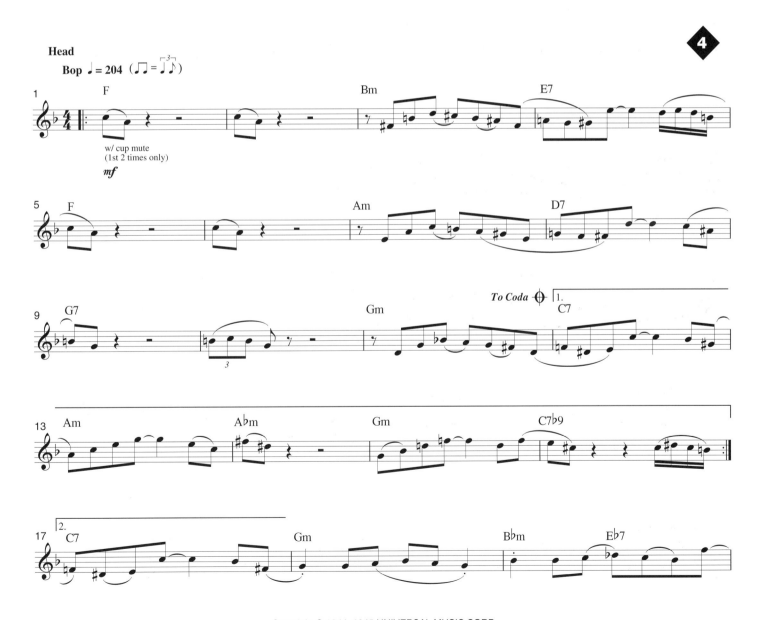

JERSEY BOUNCE
(*Dizzy Gillespie, Volume 3: 1941–1942*)
Words by Robert Wright
Music by Bobby Platter, Tiny Bradshaw, Ed Johnson and Robert Wright

Featured in the Broadway musical revue *Swing*, "Jersey Bounce" was recorded in 1942 by Les Hite and His Orchestra with Dizzy playing a solo.

After a swinging start (measures 37–40), Diz gives a two-measure taste of the double time that would characterize much of the solo work to come as a leader of his own groups. The two measures of somewhat syncopated sixteenths in measures 41–42 contain several elements of his recognizable style, including the starting of a phrase on a high note and then descending chromatically (beat 1, measure 41), diatonically (beats 2–3), and chordally (beat 4, and beat 1 of measure 42).

Notice the use of the #9 (E♭) and ♭9 (D♭) for C7 in measure 44 and the use of an F° outline for G7 (yielding the ♭7, ♭9, and 3) in measure 46. In measure 49 he uses a ♭9 chromatic passing tone on a strong beat (3), and in measure 50 E♭7 is implied—both instances over C7. Encircling chromatic neighbors (F#–E–F) complete measure 50 into the downbeat of the next measure, and measures 51 and 52 are all F with a bluesy pivot tone riff to finish. After a bridge interlude in measures 53–60, Grieg is quoted (measures 61–62), and the head is repeated (this time in the key of F), bringing the chorus to a close.

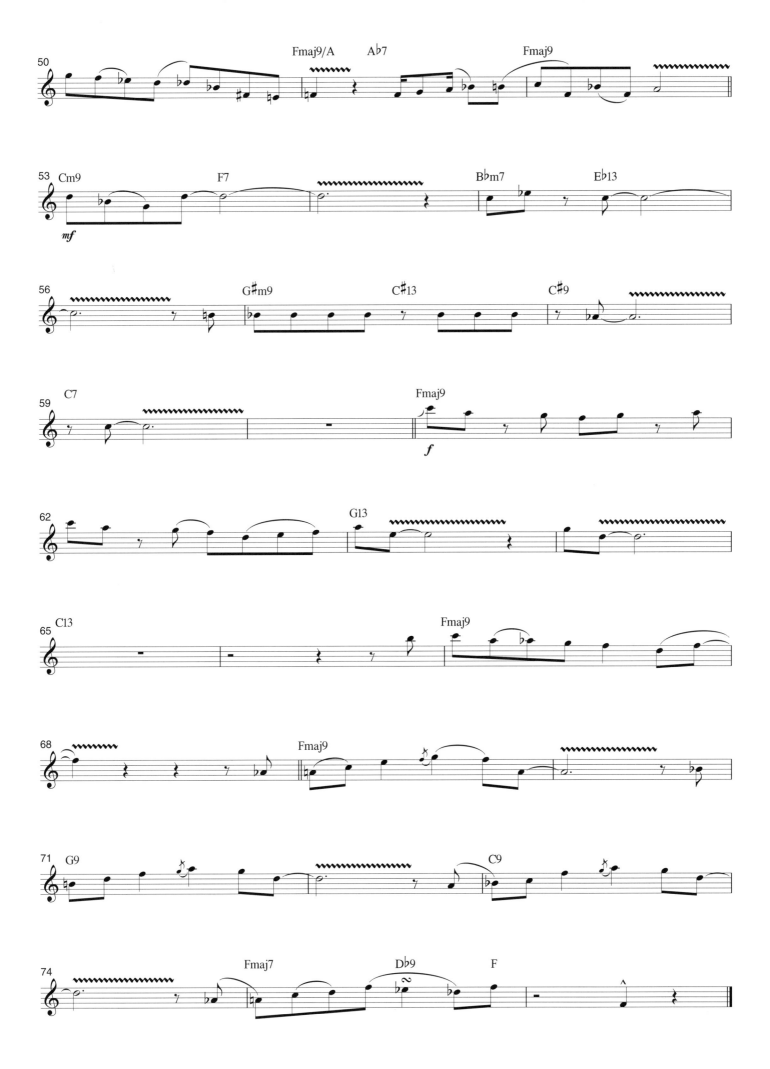

MANTECA
(*Dizzy Gillespie and His Big Band*, 1947)

By Dizzy Gillespie, Walter Gil Fuller and Luciano Pozo Gonzales

"Manteca," written in 1947 by Dizzy, Gil Fuller, and percussionist Chano Pozo, is the quintessential Afro-Cuban jazz standard. Excerpts reprinted and recorded here include Dizzy's improvisations over the tune's C7 vamp.

In measure 25, Diz characteristically begins high and descends chromatically, finishing in measure 26 with encircling chromatic neighbors (F and E♭) into E on beat 4, plus a tritone leap to the ♭7th (B♭). In measure 29, he outlines F♯+ into beat 2, then descends, first chromatically then diatonically (C Mixolydian), into a flurry of altered tones in measure 30, including the ♯5th, ♯11th, and ♯9th, ending on the ♭9th (C♯) in measure 31. Next comes an ascending B♭maj7 arpeggio into the downbeat of measure 32. After some more vamp riffs (measures 33–48), contrast is provided by the chord changes of the mellow interlude at measure 49. The bridge progression starts at measure 49 with a II–V–I in A♭. Then IV of A♭ (C♯7) moves to a V–I progression in B♭ major (Fmaj7♯11–B♭maj9). A ii–V–I return to A♭ follows, after which a false progression towards F♯ (Bm7–C♯7♭5 in measure 60) shifts to a II–V (G7♭5–C7♯11 in measures 61–62) in F. Another drive towards C major (D7♭5–G7♯11♯9 of measures 63–64) reinforces the return to the tonic vamp riff in measure 65.

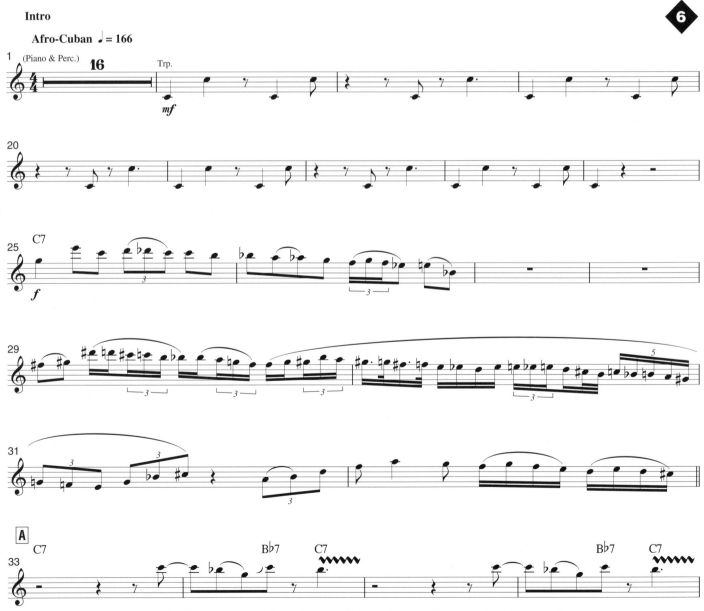

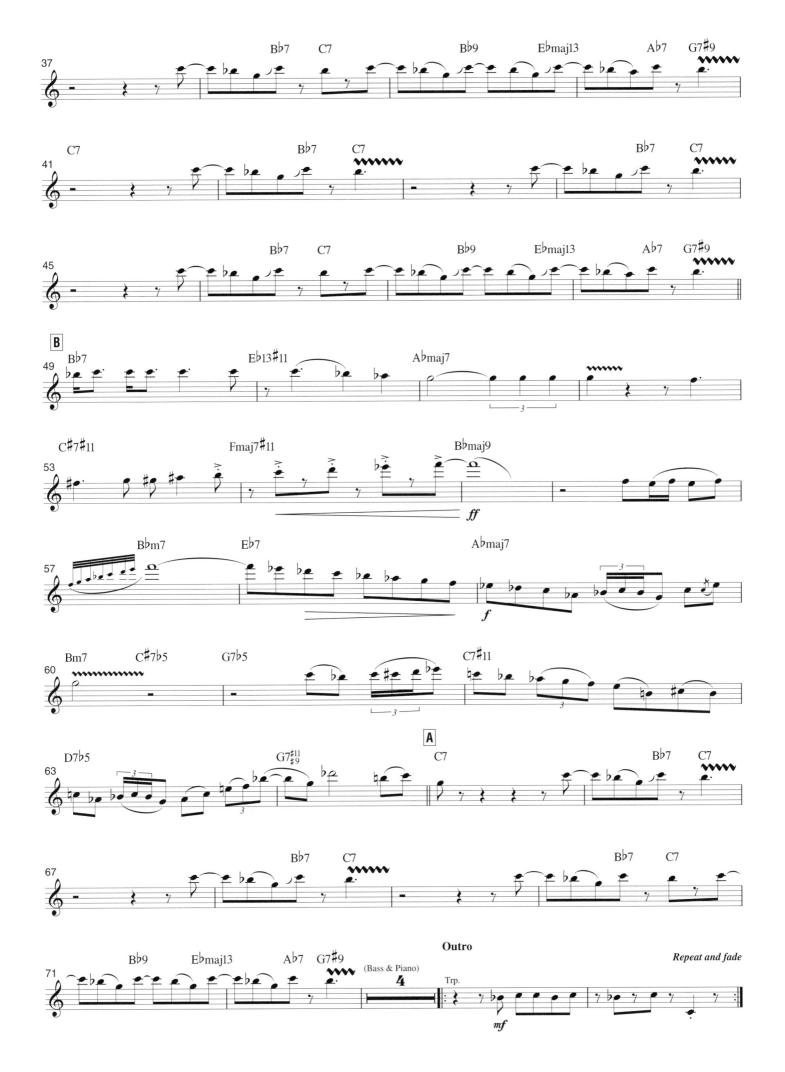

A NIGHT IN TUNISIA

(*The Complete RCA Victor Recordings: 1937–1949, 1946*)

By John "Dizzy" Gillespie and Frank Paparelli

"A Night in Tunisia," by Dizzy Gillespie and Frank Paparelli, is one of the most enduring of Dizzy's many well-known tunes. Dizzy's solo breaks (two or four measures at the end of the tag) in the many recordings and live performances of this tune are legend.

In the first solo chorus (starts measure 47), Dizzy employs encircling upper and lower chromatic neighbors (C and A♯) to get to the 5th of E minor (B) on beat 2 of measure 48. He targets the major 7th of Em9(maj7) at the end of that measure, but targets the 13th (C♯) in measure 50. In measure 51 he moves to his characteristic dazzling high register, ending the phrase with a reference to the head in measure 53.

The next section starts with more high register work featuring encircling chromatic neighbors (beats 1–2 of measure 55), diatonic material (F Mixolydian in 55 and 57), and descending chromaticism (measures 56 and 58). There is an E♭maj7 arpeggio for F13 in measure 59 and another use of the maj7th over Em9(maj7) in measure 60.

In the bridge section (starts measure 63) the ♭9th is featured for E7 in measure 64. The final eight measures (the last A section) start with an F13(♯11) to Em9(maj7) in measures 71 and 72 that is primarily superimposed as E minor. This is followed by a blistering sixteenth-note passage featuring the ♭7 and ♯5 for F13(♯11) and E Aeolian (notice the C♮) for Em9(maj7) in measures 73 and 74. The use of a C° outline (for E minor) is notable in measure 76 on the way to completion of the 32-measure form.

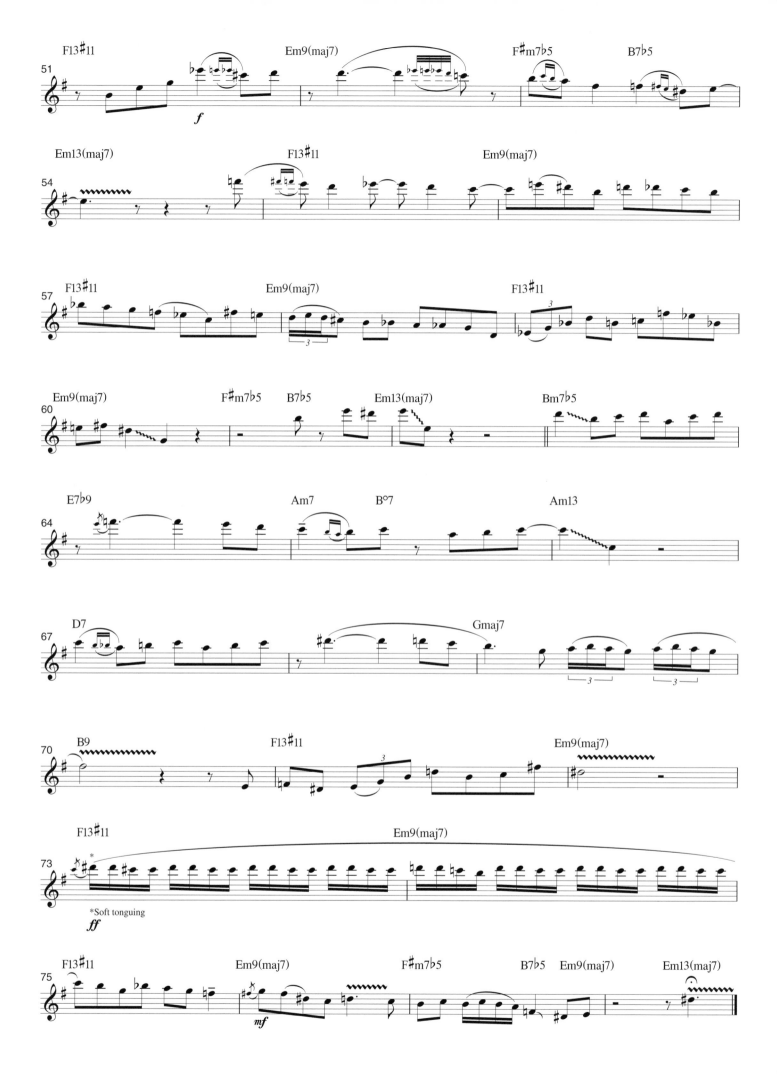

SALT PEANUTS
(*Shawnuff*, 1945)

By John "Dizzy" Gillespie and Kenny Clarke

"Salt Peanuts" was recorded by Dizzy and Bird in 1945 and featured an infectious G octave vocal riff. The composition is credited to John "Dizzy" Gillespie and drummer Kenny Clarke, and is (somewhat ironically) perhaps the most widely known of Dizzy's tunes.

After an essentially D7♭5 introduction with Diz and Bird in contrary (measures 9–13) and parallel (measures 14–15) motion, the famous head phrase repeats four times in G major. The bridge cycles through III–VI–II–V (B7–E7–A7–D7) with a sparse melody that features the ♭9th in measure 27 and 31, and the ♭5th in measures 27 and 31. The G riff returns for the last eight measures of the head (measures 34–41).

After a six-measure set up (measures 42–47), Dizzy spins off into a four-measure solo break with a swirling B♭–B–C figure followed by a scalar (G major) then chromatic descent. He finishes with an F#°7 climb (implying D7♭9). At measure 52, the solo proper commences with four solid measures of G major over the (I–ii–V) changes. Some blistering high notes in measures 57–60 set up a characteristic descent to the lower middle range (measures 61–66). Notice the use of the ♭13th (E♭) on the downbeat of measure 62.

In the bridge, Dizzy substitutes F7 for B7 in measure 69 and G major for E7 in measure 70. In measures 72–73 he employs a pivot bop riff that descends through the touchtone notes of the 5th (E), ♭5 (D#), 4th (D), and 3rd (C#). Measures 74–75 are D Mixolydian with a ♭5 (A♭) chromatic passing tone. Notice the targeted 9th for G major at the downbeat of measure 76 and the isolated ♭5 (G#) for D7 in measure 77. There are nice chromatic passing tones in measures 79–80, including a ♭13th for D7 and G7 (B♭ and E♭, respectively), as well as a ♭5th on beat 3 for G7 in measure 80. The ♭5th starts the C in measure 81, and encircling chromatic neighbors (C and A# in measure 82) occur in the final G major phrase of the solo.

SHAWNUFF
(*Shawnuff*, 1945)

By Charlie Parker and John "Dizzy" Gillespie

"Shawnuff" is another Dizzy classic, co-composed with Charlie Parker for their 1945 recordings.

The solo starts with a diatonic flourish up to a 5th. Dizzy plays a "bebop scale" (G Mixolydian with major 7 passing tone) all the way through measure 55 and 56 extending into measure 57 (where it becomes a C major scale). The D harmonic minor scale gets into A7 (♭9 implied) in measure 63, and an Fmaj7 arpeggio (for Dm7) into the ♯5th of G7 completes the passage in measure 64. Measure 66 has a D7 outline for the F♯°7 chord, and measure 67 features lower and upper chromatic neighbors around the 3rd of C.

In the bridge of these "rhythm changes," two notes, the 13th and ♯11th, suffice for the A7 measures (71–72). The bop idea in measure 74 (beginning on beat 2) is mirrored in measure 76. Dm7 to G7 is substituted in the G7 measures (75–76). There is a good amount of variation in the triplets of measures 77–78. Dizzy gets to the F♯°7 right away in measure 82. He switches from the major 7th in measure 83 to the ♭7th in measure 84 for the C chords.

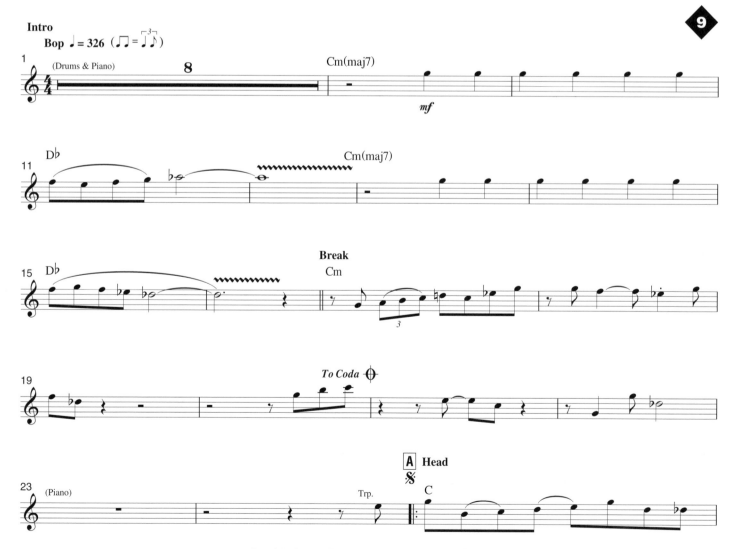

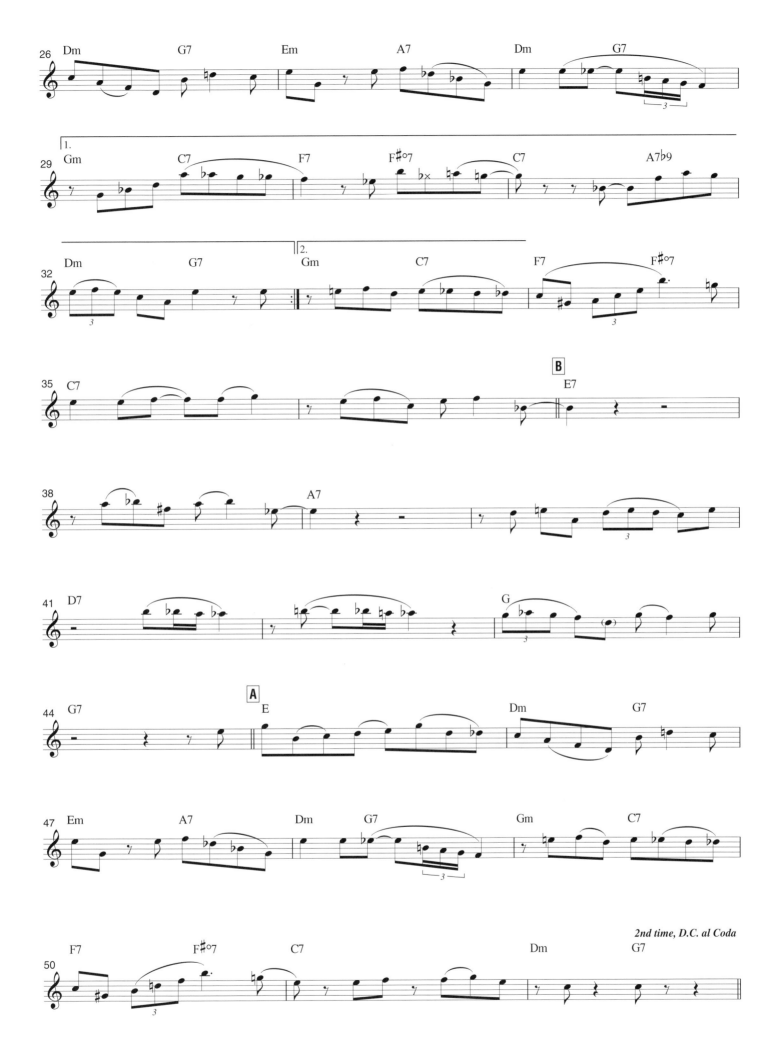

STELLA BY STARLIGHT
(*Birk's Works: Verve Big Band Sessions*, 1956)

Words by Ned Washington
Music by Victor Young

Victor Young's "Stella by Starlight" (from the film *The Uninvited*) received a reworked head and a nice solo from Dizzy. The use of space (measure 10), displaced melody (measure 17), and certain melodic motifs (measure 27) evoke fellow trumpeter Miles Davis, who also did numerous reinterpretations of this classic tune.

The lead-in to the solo (measures 29–32) makes good use of altered 9ths (A♭ to B♭ for G7) and encircling chromatic neighbors (A♭ and F♯ to G at the downbeat of measure 32). In the second half of measure 33, Dizzy anticipates B7 with a descending A° outline. A nice chromatic phrase lands on B (♭5th of F) at the downbeat of measure 39. C is anticipated in the second half of measure 40 and also serves to feature the ♯11th and 13th of the B♭7 chord. An E Locrian ♯2 scale swirls through measure 43 to the ♭9–♯9–♭5 phrase ending in measure 44 for A7, followed by a reference to the head. The E♭ Lydian figure in measures 46–47 (for the B7 and Bm7♭5 chords) is further emphasized by the space that follows it.

The second half of measure 50 implies the tritone substitution E♭7 for the A7 chord. The rotating F–E–C figure in measures 52–55 is inspired, as is the shift of the A♭ from that passage to the A♮ of its resolution (to C6) in measure 56. B7 is again anticipated in an F♯m7♭5 measure (57), and the ♭9 is featured in both the Em7♭5 and A7 measures (59 and 60). G7 gets a Lydian ♭7 mode in measure 62.

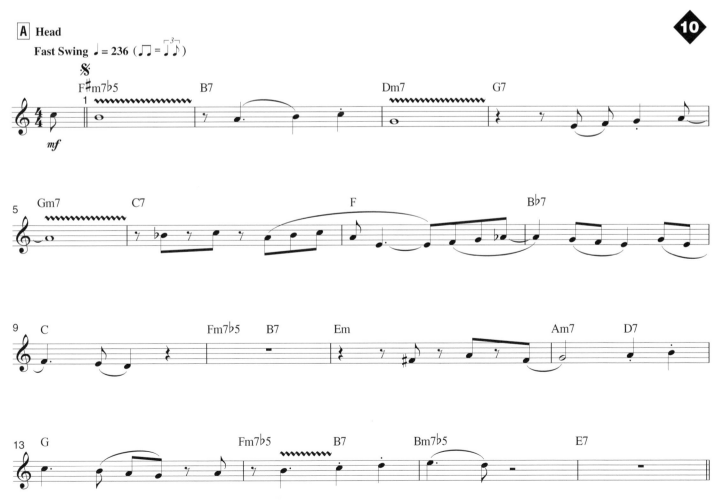

TOUR DE FORCE
(*Birk's Works: Verve Big Band Sessions*, 1956)

By John "Dizzy" Gillespie

A seldom-mentioned Dizzy composition, "Tour de Force" is deceptively simple with its gently descending chromatic bass progression that works its way down to B♭ major and its ii–V–I bridge at measure 17, half in E♭ (IV) and half in F (V). A ten-measure extension (measure 33–42) sets up the solos, which begin with a one-measure break (last measure of the extension).

Dizzy's solo is all about B♭ major from the break through the first four chromatic changes (measures 42–44). Measure 45 is an altered F bebop dominant scale (1–2–3–4–5–6–♭7–♮7) where the 6th is lowered by a half step (D♭ in beat 2). There is a nice substitution in the second half of measure 46 that implies G7♯9 and leads like a V–i to Em7♭5 (which is C9 in disguise) in measure 47. Dizzy treats measures 47–48 like a ii–V–I in B♭ despite the chromatic changes (same treatment in 49–50 where it is expected). Measures 51–52 get a seemingly more individual treatment of each chord change, although all the notes come from the B♭ major scale (except the A♭ for D♭m7 in measure 52). Notice the delayed arrival of B♭ tonality in measure 54 (on beat 2) after an extension of F7 (V chord) in beat 1, utilizing the ♭9 (F♯) and ♯9 (G♯). The last four-measure phrase before the bridge is all B♭ major.

In the bridge, Dizzy goes into his famous syncopated sixteenth-note double time style. He gets the most out of each chord by using chromatic devices such as root–7th–♭7th for F minor in measure 59 and the encircling chromatic neighbors (C♯ and B to C) in measure 60. There is also use of chord outlining (F minor in measure 61), cascading and ascending scales (measures 62 and 63), and altered tone shifts (♯4 to 4 for C7 in measure 63, and major 7 to ♭7 in measure 64). Dizzy goes ultra high (measures 66–67) to get out of the bridge and back to single time. A bluesy B♭ major treatment takes good care of the final eight measures of the solo chorus (67–74).

WOODYN' YOU
(*Rainbow Mist*, 1944)

By Dizzy Gillespie

Many consider Dizzy's composition "Woodyn' You" to be the first bebop tune. It was written for a February 1944 Coleman Hawkins recording session and is constructed of interlocking, descending ii–V progressions into the tonic E♭ major (measures 1–8). The bridge (measures 9–16) consists of essentially two sets of ii–V progressions—in A♭ (IV) and B♭ (V).

Dizzy's solo starts (measure 25) with a leading tone pick-up note (B) into a C minor outline that jumps to the 9th of C minor (11th of Am7♭5) and then descends, in effect using C minor for Am7♭5. A bop riff in measure 26 utilizes F♯°7 to get the 3rd, 5th, ♭7th, and ♭9th of D7. C7♯9 is anticipated in measure 27 with the E♭ on beat 3. The ♭9th is heard in measure 30 (B♭7) and 31 (E♭maj7) where the melody is referenced. An altered dominant scale, D Mixolydian ♭6 (the fifth mode of G melodic minor), is used in measure 34, and encircling chromatic neighbors (F and E♭) to the 3rd (E) are found in measure 36 for C7. Dizzy rips down from 7th to 4th for the Fm7♭5 in measure 37 and anticipates E♭maj7 in the following B♭7 measure (38).

In the bridge, Dizzy starts high with his characteristic descent using first chromatic then diatonic scales. The ♯5th and ♭5th are featured for E♭7 in measure 43 and also serve as encircling chromatic neighbors to A♭maj7's 9th on the downbeat of measure 44. A Dizzying rotating chromatic riff drills through measure 45–46, descending through measure 47 into the ♭9 (B♮) of B♭13 in measure 48. The ♭6th appears in a D dominant scale again in measure 50, and G Locrian ♯2 (the sixth mode of B♭ melodic minor) descends through measure 51 for Gm7♭5. A triplet outline up C9 from 3rd to 9th (E to D) in measure 52 leads to a descending F Locrian scale in measure 53. The ♭9th is again used for B♭7 (measure 54), and an E♭6 outline (first half of measure 55) leads to encircling chromatic neighbors (A♭ and F♯) into the 3rd (G) in the solo's concluding phrase.

D.C. al Coda
(take repeat)

Trumpet Notation Legend

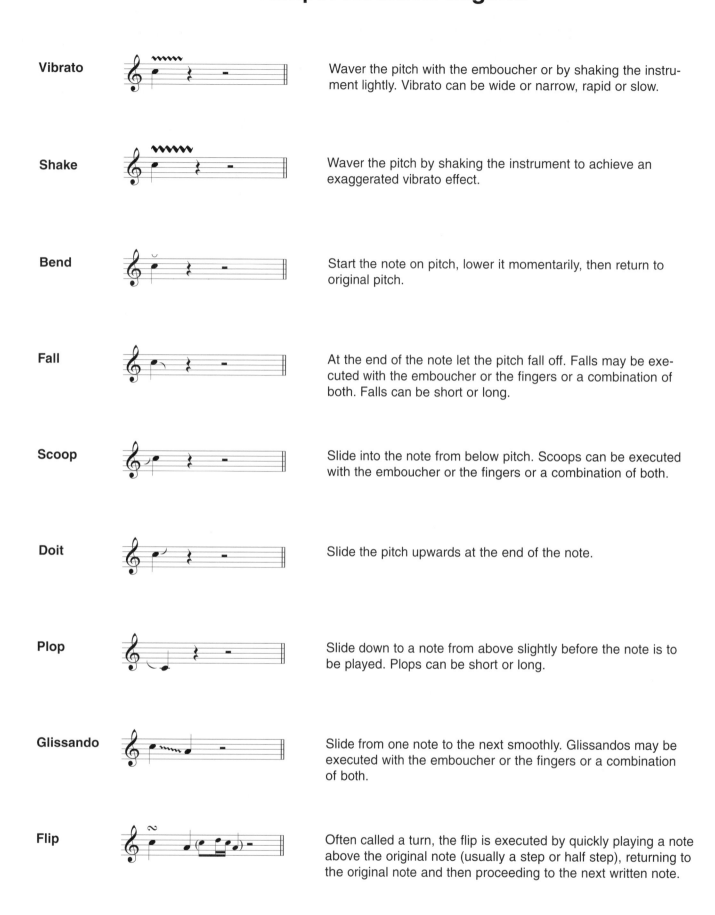

Vibrato — Waver the pitch with the emboucher or by shaking the instrument lightly. Vibrato can be wide or narrow, rapid or slow.

Shake — Waver the pitch by shaking the instrument to achieve an exaggerated vibrato effect.

Bend — Start the note on pitch, lower it momentarily, then return to original pitch.

Fall — At the end of the note let the pitch fall off. Falls may be executed with the emboucher or the fingers or a combination of both. Falls can be short or long.

Scoop — Slide into the note from below pitch. Scoops can be executed with the emboucher or the fingers or a combination of both.

Doit — Slide the pitch upwards at the end of the note.

Plop — Slide down to a note from above slightly before the note is to be played. Plops can be short or long.

Glissando — Slide from one note to the next smoothly. Glissandos may be executed with the emboucher or the fingers or a combination of both.

Flip — Often called a turn, the flip is executed by quickly playing a note above the original note (usually a step or half step), returning to the original note and then proceeding to the next written note.